Dedicated to Possibility

Published by: Ai Candi
Written and Illustrated by: Aileen Joy
Reviewed by: Melissa Pallister
Edited by: Blythe Thimsen
ISBN: 978-0-578-74545-9

Bring it Back to Simple

Art, Thoughts and Poems, Volume 1

Root yourself so deep in your purpose
nothing can pull you from it.

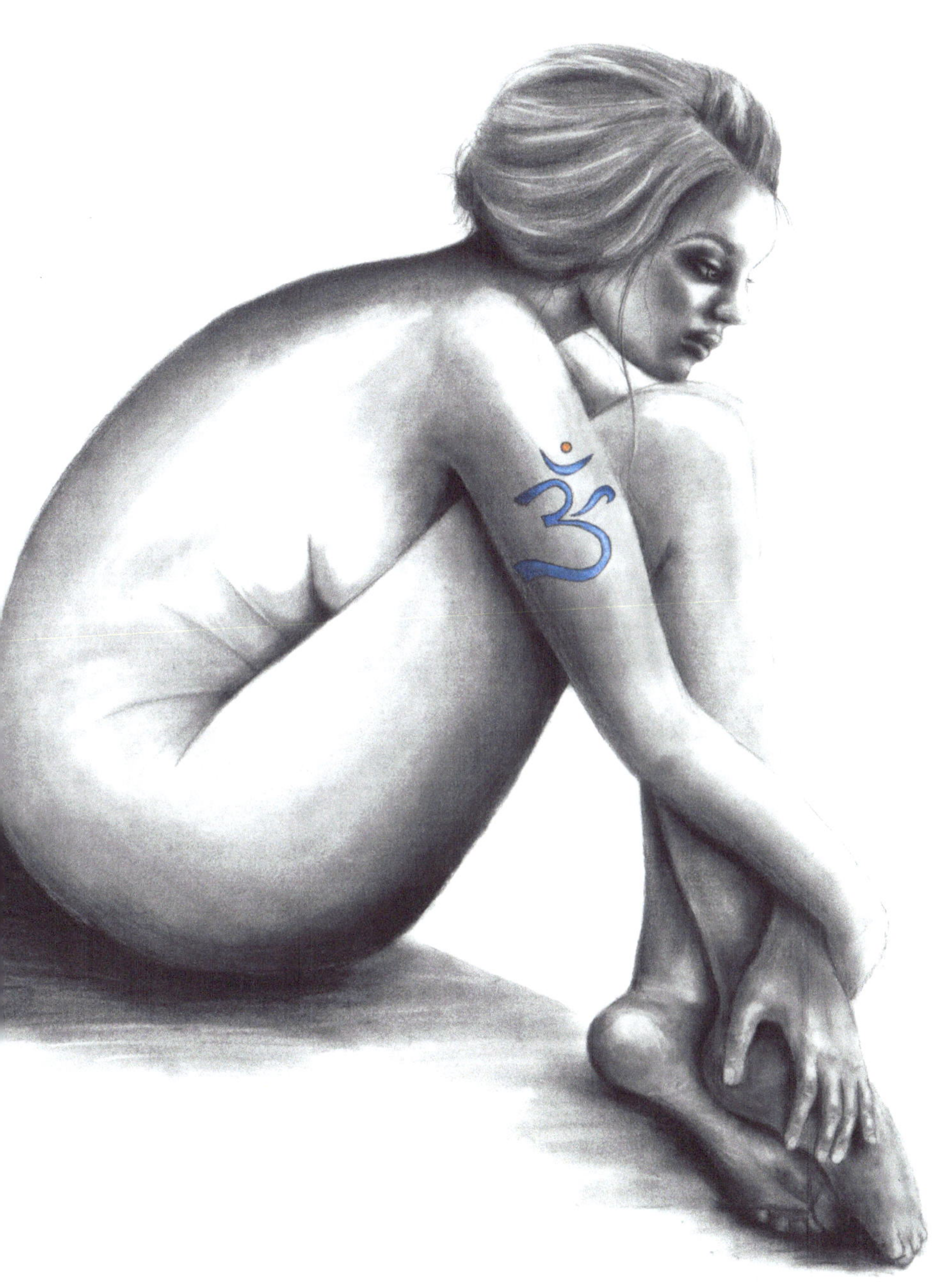

My soul defines me,
my imagination sculpts me,
and the ones I love inspire me.

Where will raw artisans be in 50 years?
Will they be swept into dusty corners as technology replaces the very soul of humanity?

Love to the fullest,
be gentle with yourself,
and remember to always make art,
however that may be.

Painted Dreams

I shut my eyes, imagining the places I could be
what beautiful things I could see,
different people I would meet
as I walk along a cobblestone street,
buildings themselves a work of art
my eyes following every sculpted part,
painters everywhere I turn
oh the things from them I could learn,
the smell of spices linger in the air
accented by the sun's bright glare,
clotheslines drooping window to window
the wind ripples through them with each gentle blow,
I keep walking along
birds fly by singing a sweet song,
as I look around, I sit down
gazing at this meadow-framed town,
with white lilies and blue butterflies
the sky above splashed with exotic dyes,
as the colors melt away
it ends this wishful day,
I open my eyes from the dream
my soul left with a pleasant gleam,
someday I will find this place
I say to myself, with a smiling face.

The Earth is a reflection of us.
The oil its blood, the trees its breath, and the crust its flesh.
We have harvested its body beyond repair and polluted it
with its own resources and our twisted inventions.
Just like any of us, being overused and malnourished
become sick, so has the earth.
This is not sustainable, and without change
it will soon become another empty planet in the galaxy.

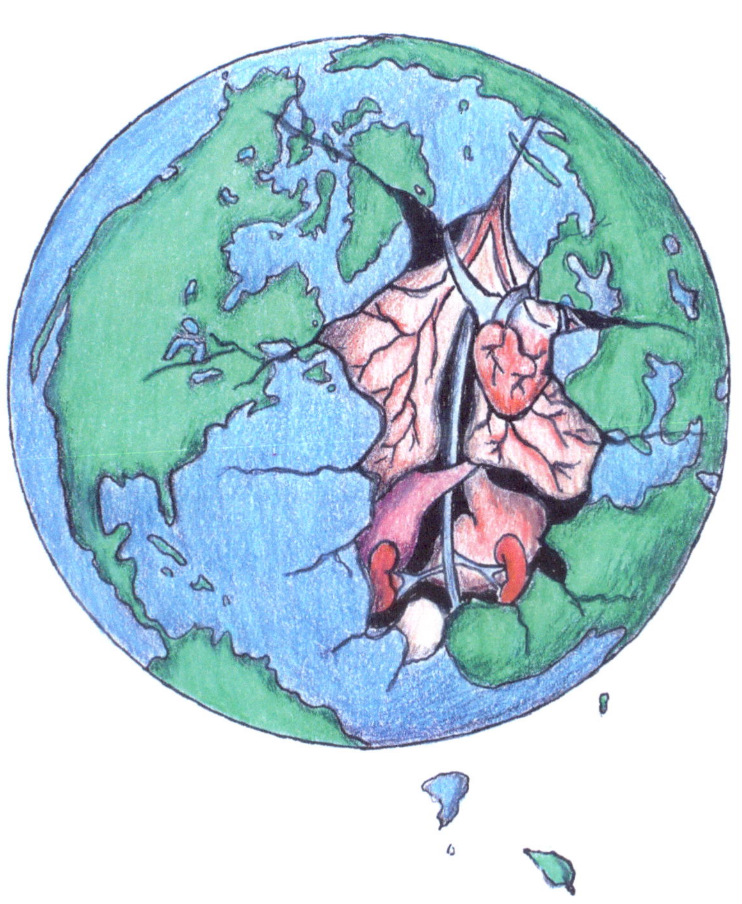

In an effort to eradicate racism, sexism, stereotyping and discrimination, people are creating more of it by assigning it to places that it never existed.

The power of today is the ability to self-educate.
What an intense freedom. Hold on to it.

I can't escape this dark side of your mind,
I painfully cry oceans and try to swim out,
I desperately grasp a hold and try to climb out,
I even call for you with all that I am,
but the depths are so deep that you can't hear me.

If everyone found something negative
which they are passionate about altering,
and fueled solutions to share a message,
the collective actions would drastically change the world.

Inhabit your days with wonder;
expectations smother out gratitude.

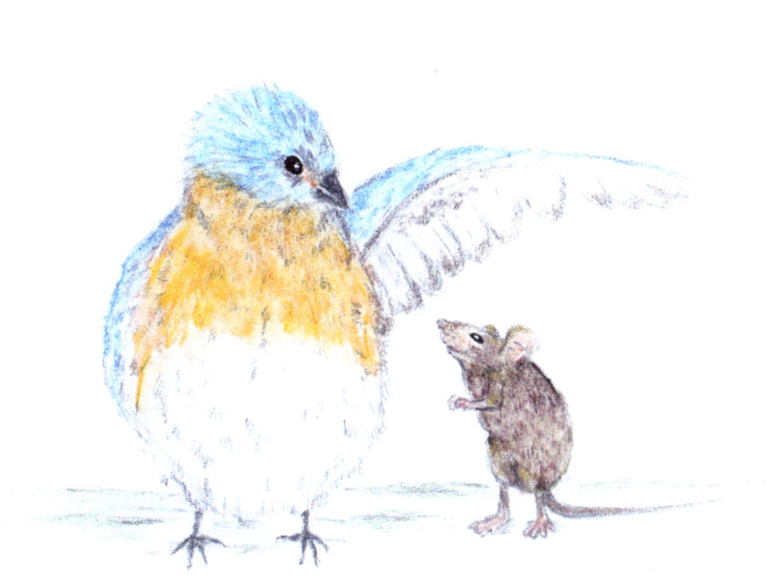

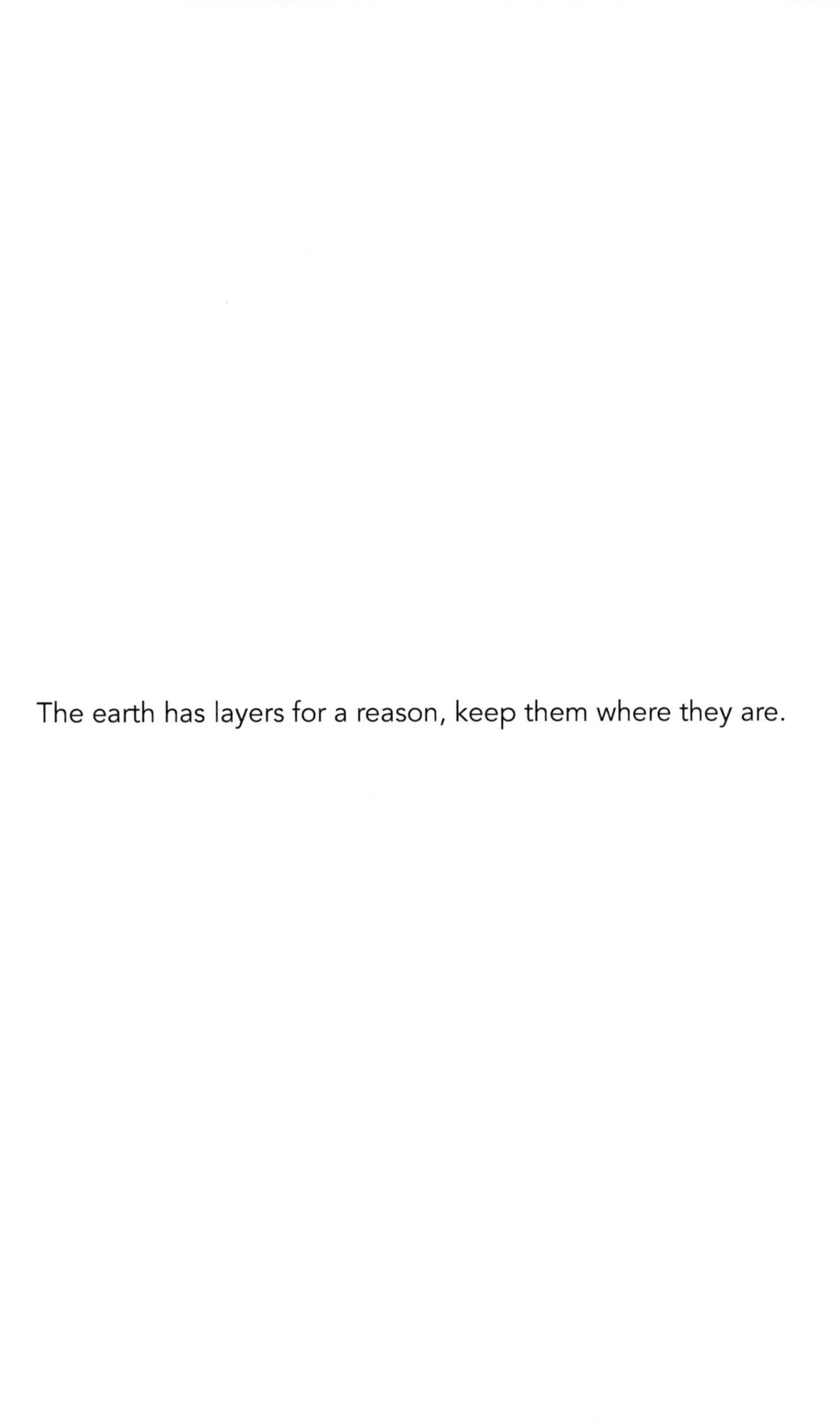

The earth has layers for a reason, keep them where they are.

Everything is connected in the world;
people, trees, animals, all living things
we are linked in a chain of existence.
Could it be one of the reasons people
are becoming less connected?
Because pieces of the chain
are breaking away into extinction?

History repeats itself...
Not necessarily because lack of knowing history,
but because of selfishness.
It will always manifest the same results,
the same wars and broken relationships,
sequentially degrading society and the earth.

As I gaze at our American flag flapping in the wind
I have a deep feeling of despair,
remembering Miss Liberty's words secured to her stone,
only to see them forgotten by leaders and followers.
Watching the progress we've made being slowly taken,
I cling to America's progressive integrity and honor,
the hope of continued change is rooted within my soul.
America has been taken hostage by corrupt corporations,
crooked politicians and the ignorance of many.
I feel its intense struggle to be set free again,
trying to grasp what it once dreamed of.
I can only have the hope it will.

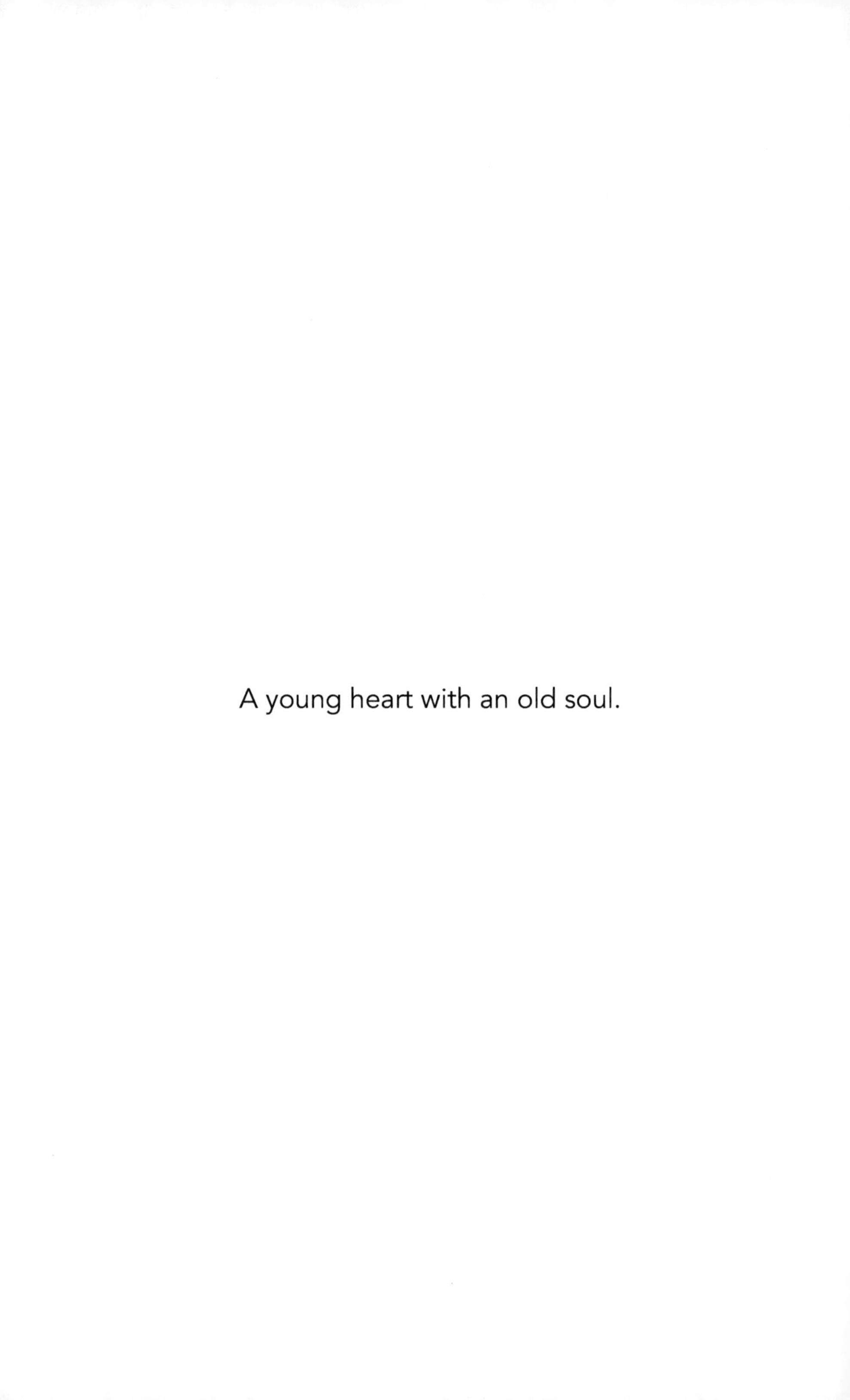

A young heart with an old soul.

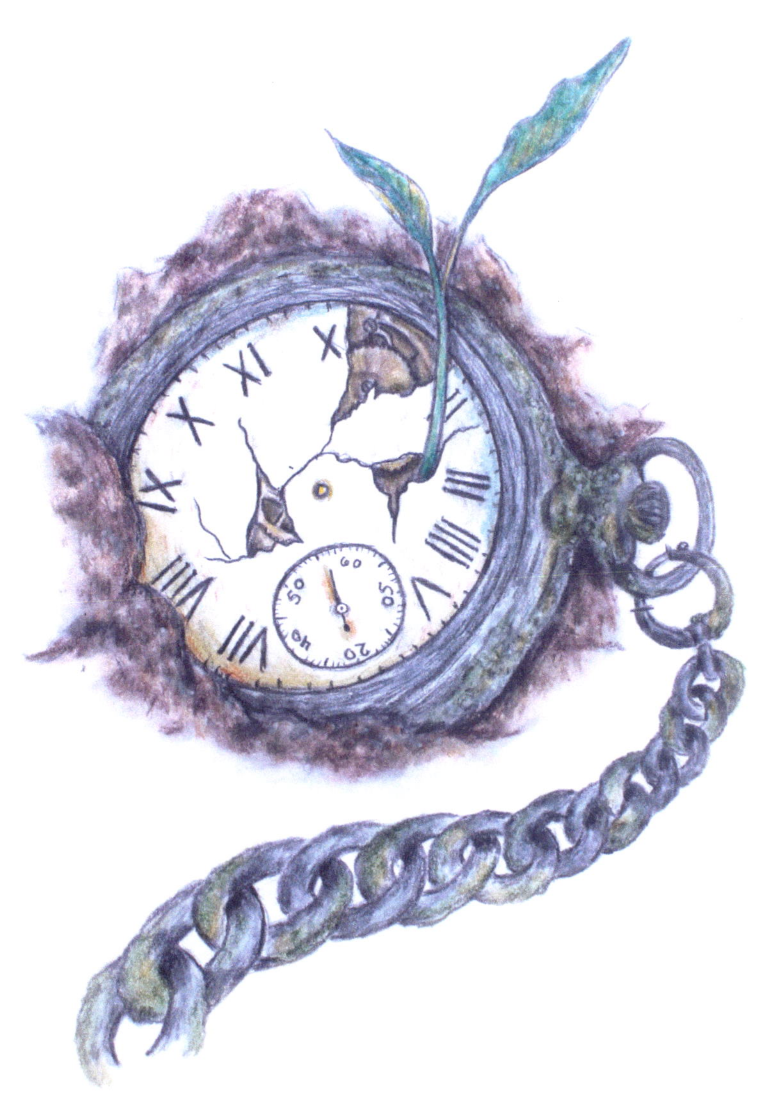

I constantly feel like I'm falling and I don't know why.

How can I keep seeing you as beautiful
when you treat me so ugly?

I'm a gentle soul,
why must my words be illy reproduced?
There's nothing to prove here,
because I am not right nor wrong;
just simple, transparent,
wanting understanding, nothing more.

Anxiety cracked open; walking on proverbial egg shells
based on internal preconceived worries,
hindering the extremes you're truly capable of.

I am in love with you, not any person of the past.
Never would it make sense you to pay for their mistakes,
you are your own, not anyone else.
I will travel the ups and downs of our terrain,
leaving the conquered valleys behind,
making our roots stronger.

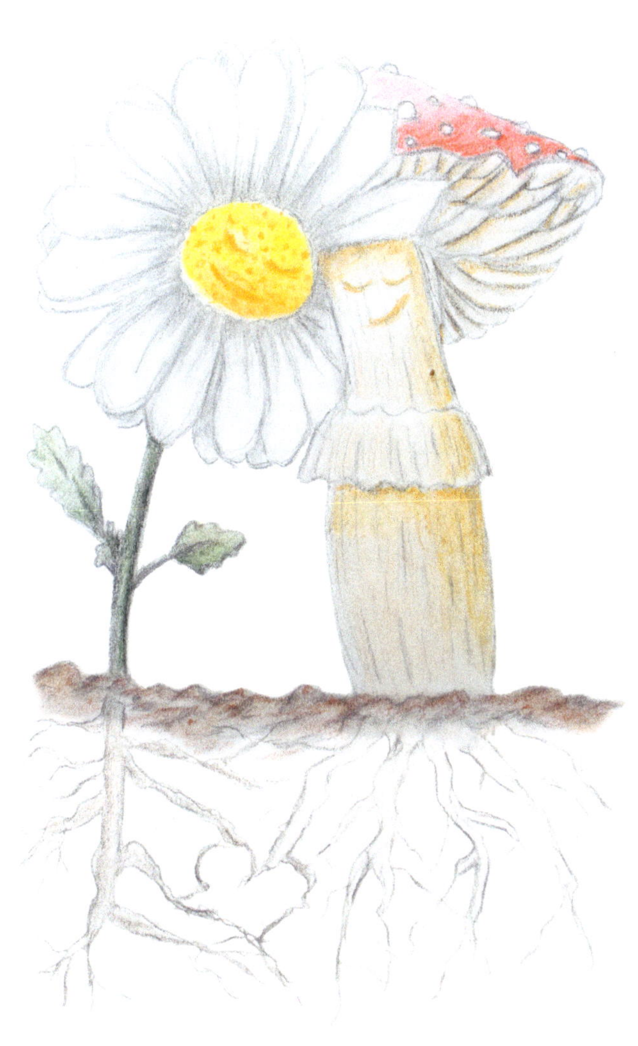

Don’t reduce me, I’m not a gravy.
I’m a human being with a beating heart.

Not all women are maternal in the stereotypical sense,
yet it's as if they break a sacred law if they choose
not to have a child. Realize they are just as valuable,
a different sort of mother to people
and other things in this world.

I feel the closest to God when I step out of the busy world
into nature, it has saved me in many ways,
I wish I could return the favor.

When did I change my mind?
I didn’t change my mind,
I realized my mind never changed.

You know yourself, your thoughts, dreams, questions and everything in between. Don't let the outside mold you into something that's so unfamiliar to who you are.

Life is just a whisper in time,
be with the ones you love.

Live light hearted.

The more rigid you are, the less give life has.

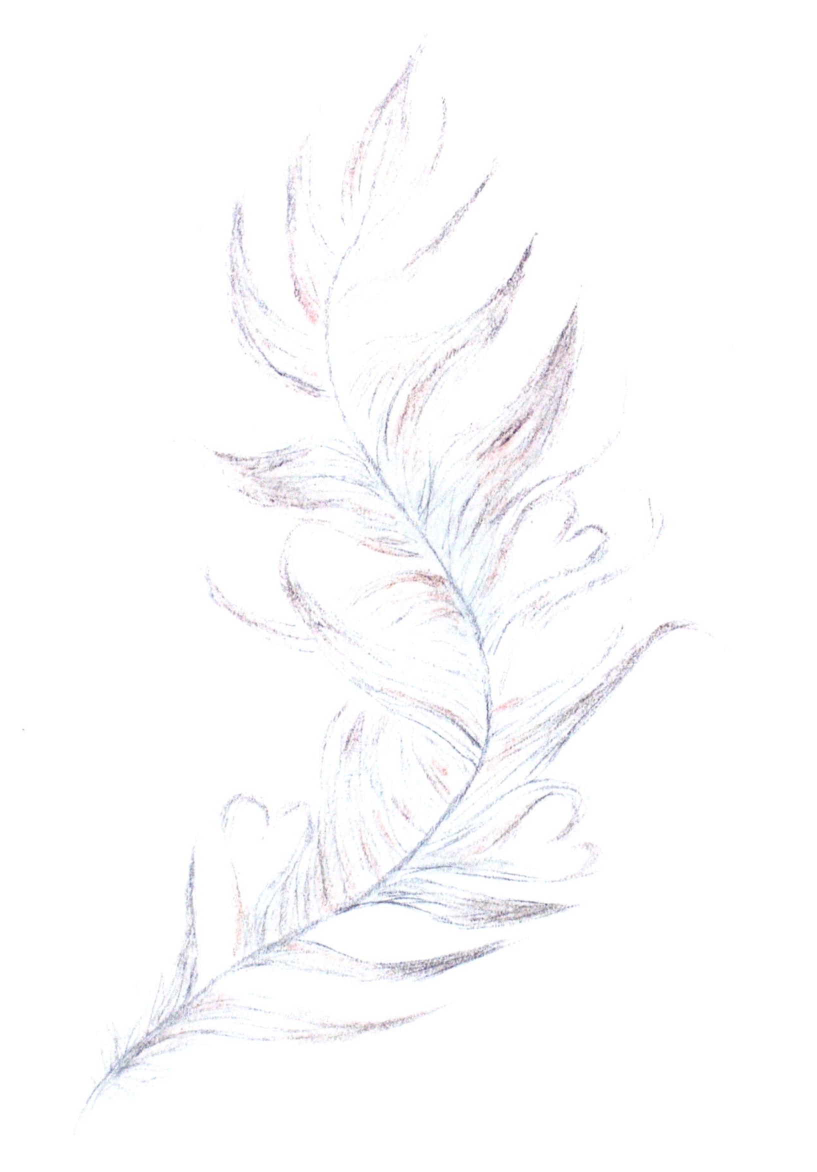

Shuffled Years

Photo albums were tucked away
for those sad times like today,
when I want to remember
but soon wish to forget,
it's painful to know
I had to let you go,
my innocence, my pride
the past life that died,
I miss that naïve bliss
that once honest kiss,
such a deep empty pain
staying busy to remain sane,
nothing to do but stay fast, don't think
hide my tears with every blink,
destiny is blind
always changing its mind.

We are on a social platform now
where selfless deeds are done for self-promotion.

I don’t want to be cataloged and filed into
the retired section of your library,
I have so many more chapters.

Bucket list...

Run my fingers across the bunches of grapes
in an Italian vineyard.

Dip my toes in an ocean that's so clean
you can't tell the water from air.

Be spitting distance from a camel in Egypt.

Have the spices touch my tongue
straight from a plate in India.

Walk along a street where every person
is treated with respect, regardless of stature.

Sit in the middle of the Sistine Chapel,
to have the paintings and history saturate my very core.

Things that are tangible and real
are being substituted with virtualization.
Relationships, books, art, music, businesses...time.
Leaving us yearning for the magic that once was.

Why do you reach for that empty bottle
when I’m right here full of love?

Naiveness should be met with education;
maliciousness should be met with intolerance.
There is a difference, don't confuse them.

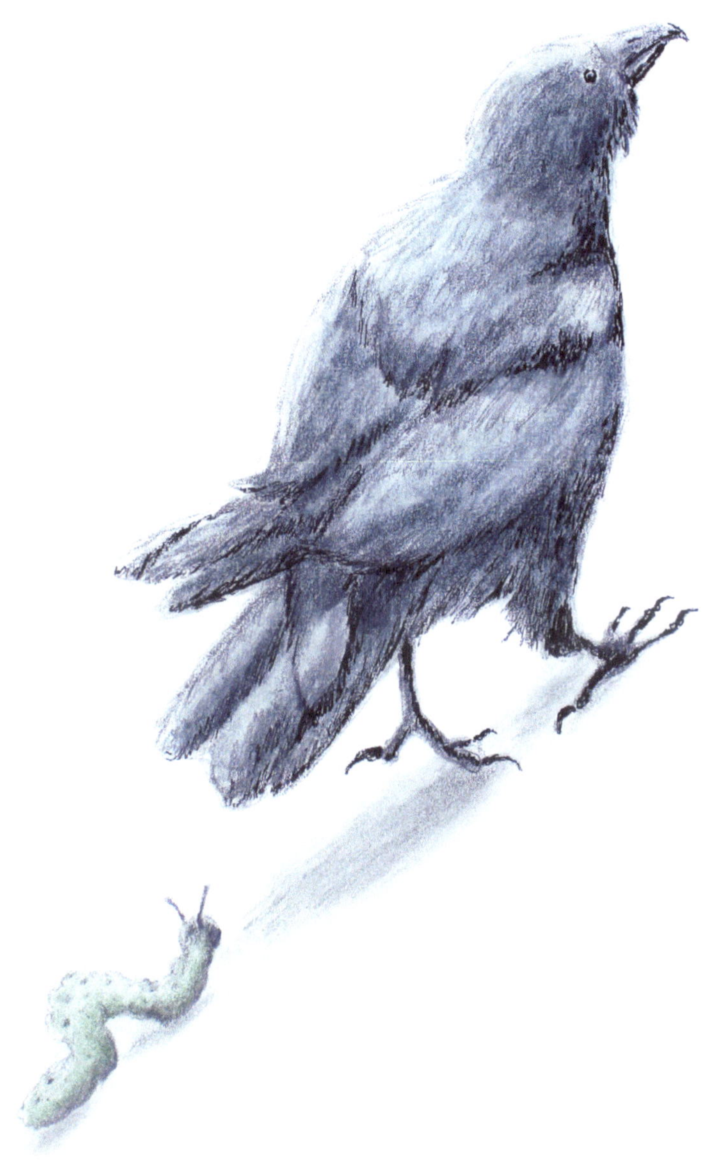

The more you try to not be yourself,
the more awkward it gets.

This world wasn't meant to be so complicated.
Just be, no need to define.
Remove labels from yourselves and others, and simply love.
We are all flesh and bones harboring a soul.

You were poison disguised as a breath of freedom;
my body frantically gasped for the stolen exhale.

Perception is your own, that does not make it truth.

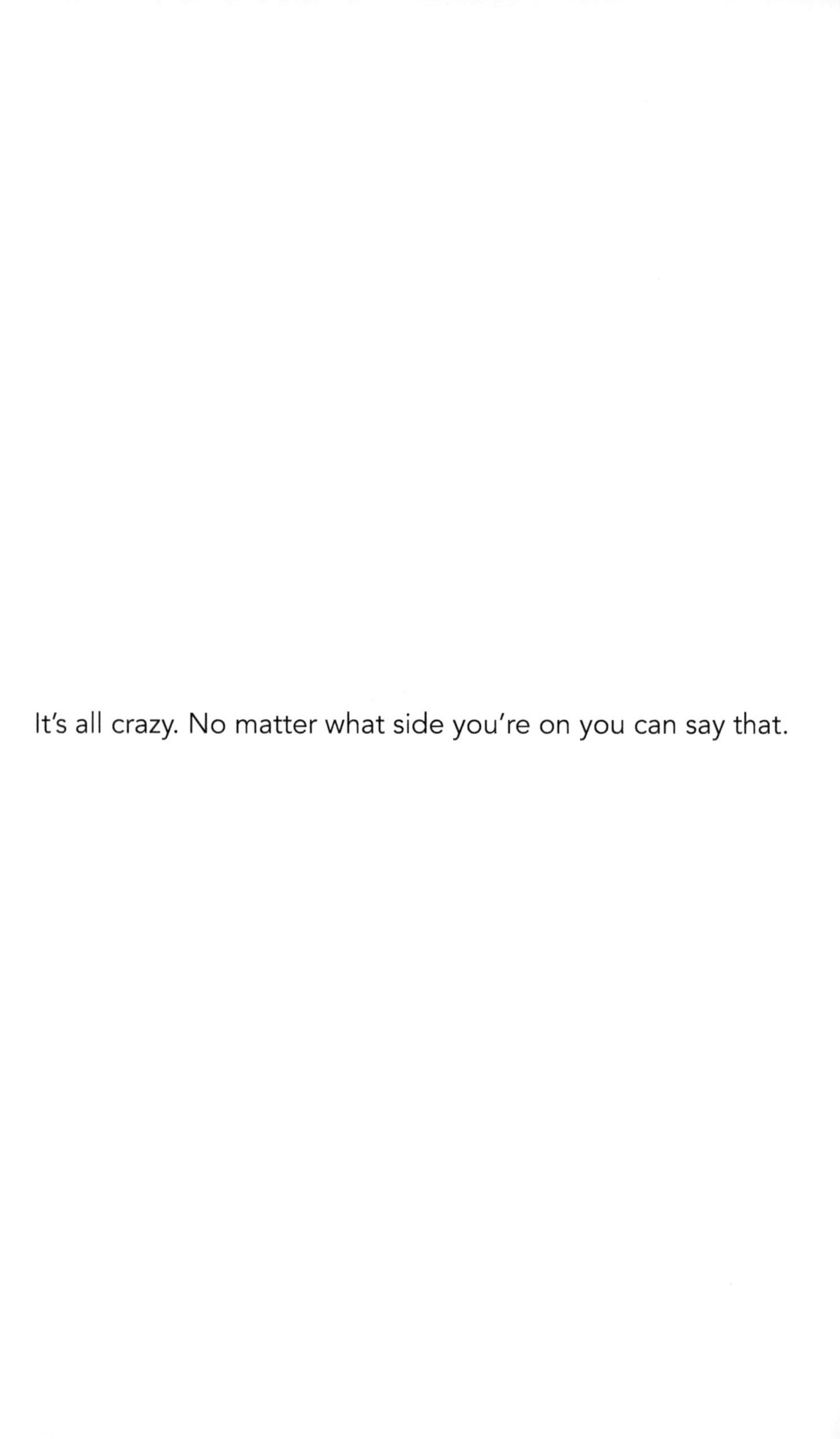

It’s all crazy. No matter what side you’re on you can say that.

You can know someone for a lifetime
without knowing them at all.

I don't think walls represent America very well.
When I think of freedom, I see endless landscapes
connected by oceans.

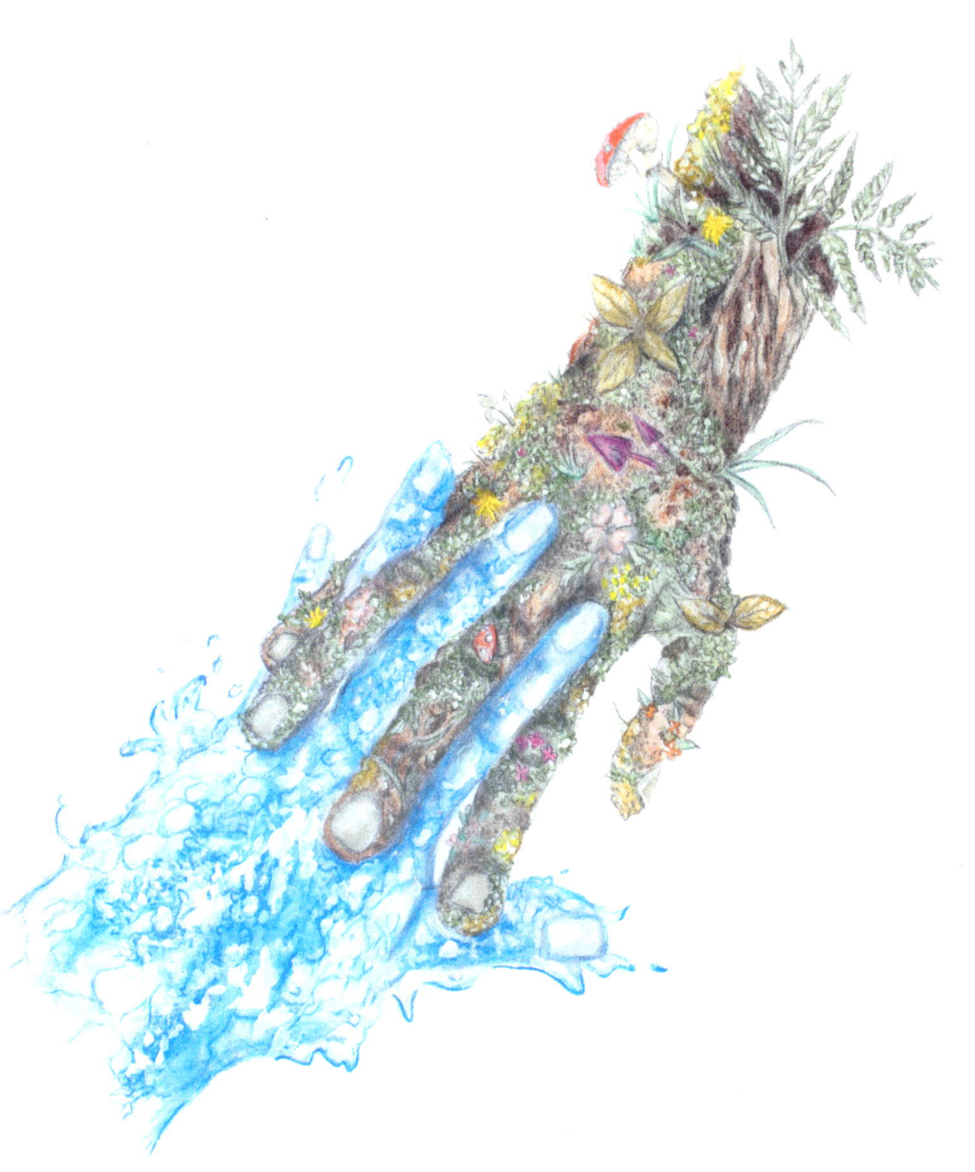

I used to be a tree with so many leaves,
bearing across seasons and the eves,
but over time I became more bare,
until one year my leaves were no longer there.

The only thing you leave with is your soul,
so make it a good one.

She stood in front of it all, decided to let go,
and she was free.

"Shopping list gone askew"

Oranges
Bananas
Pickles
Romaine
Rome
Europe
Passport
Travel guide
Travel bag
Reserve Airbnb
Buy plane tickets
Send "peace out" texts
Live!

If you have lost yourself,
dismantle the life you've comfortably created.

The phrase "That's not my job"
only creates more gaps in progress and society.

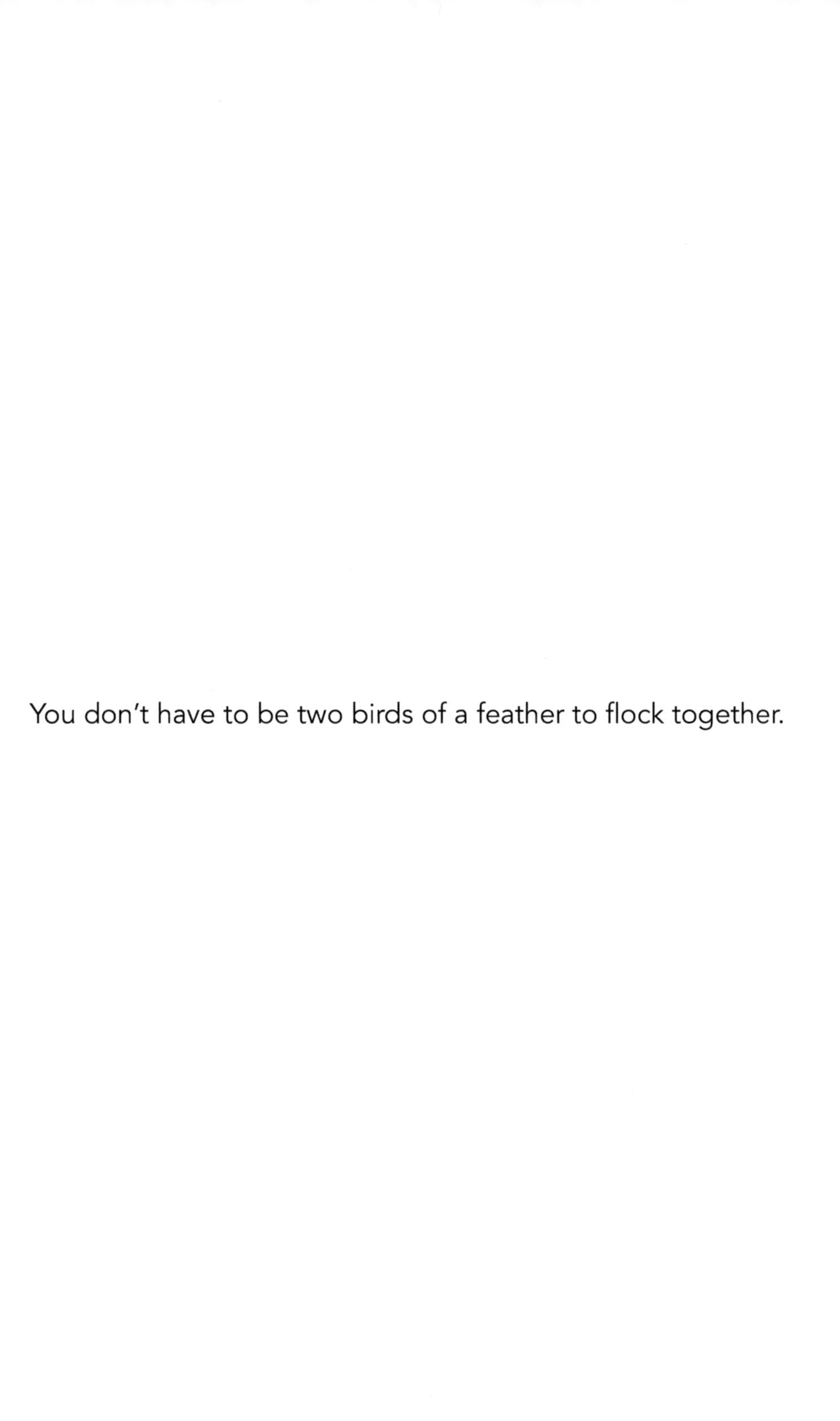

You don't have to be two birds of a feather to flock together.

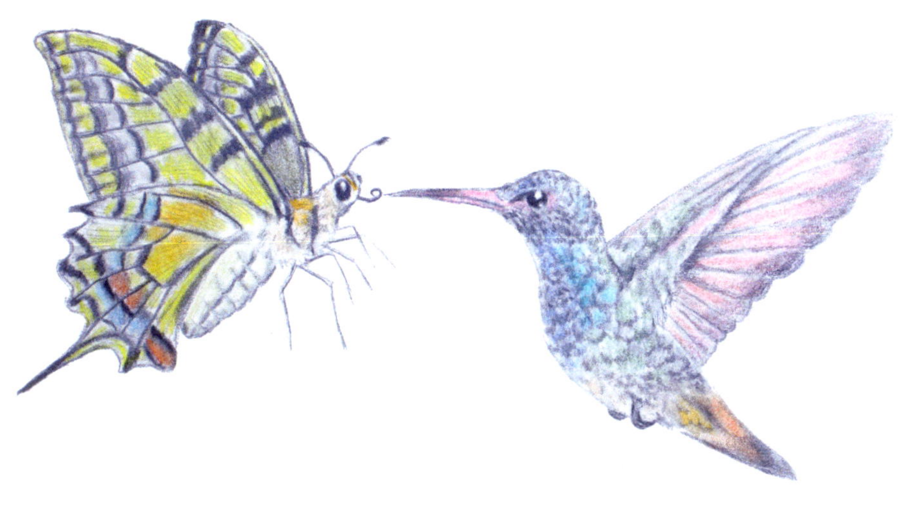

The less connected we are to Earth,
the more lost we become.

I don’t want to string my own art across my walls.
Why would I do that when they live in my thoughts?
Show me the colors of other minds.

Counting sheep.
My sheep rock mullets and jump over rings of fire.
It's much more fun that way,
but also may be the reason I have insomnia.

There's a vulnerability in the arts.
Maybe that's why it's so prized by some
and discarded by others.
Those who have empathy and connection feel it,
and those who do not, have no need for it.

You can't hold on to someone who has already let you go.
Let go, shedding all the reasons you so desperately seek.

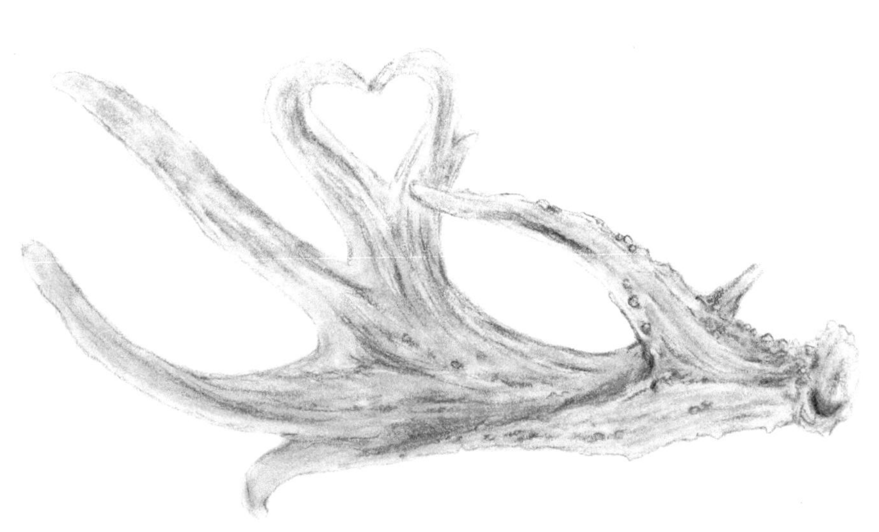

There may be many reasons you feel unfree,
but being trapped in uncertainty may be among the worst.

Some people don't believe global warming is real.
Either way, there is something that is very real,
and that's the polluted water from our processes,
suffocating animals from our garbage,
reduced oxygen from our smog,
and ecosystems being wiped away due to our conduct.

So please explain your argument again
of why it's okay to keep these habits.

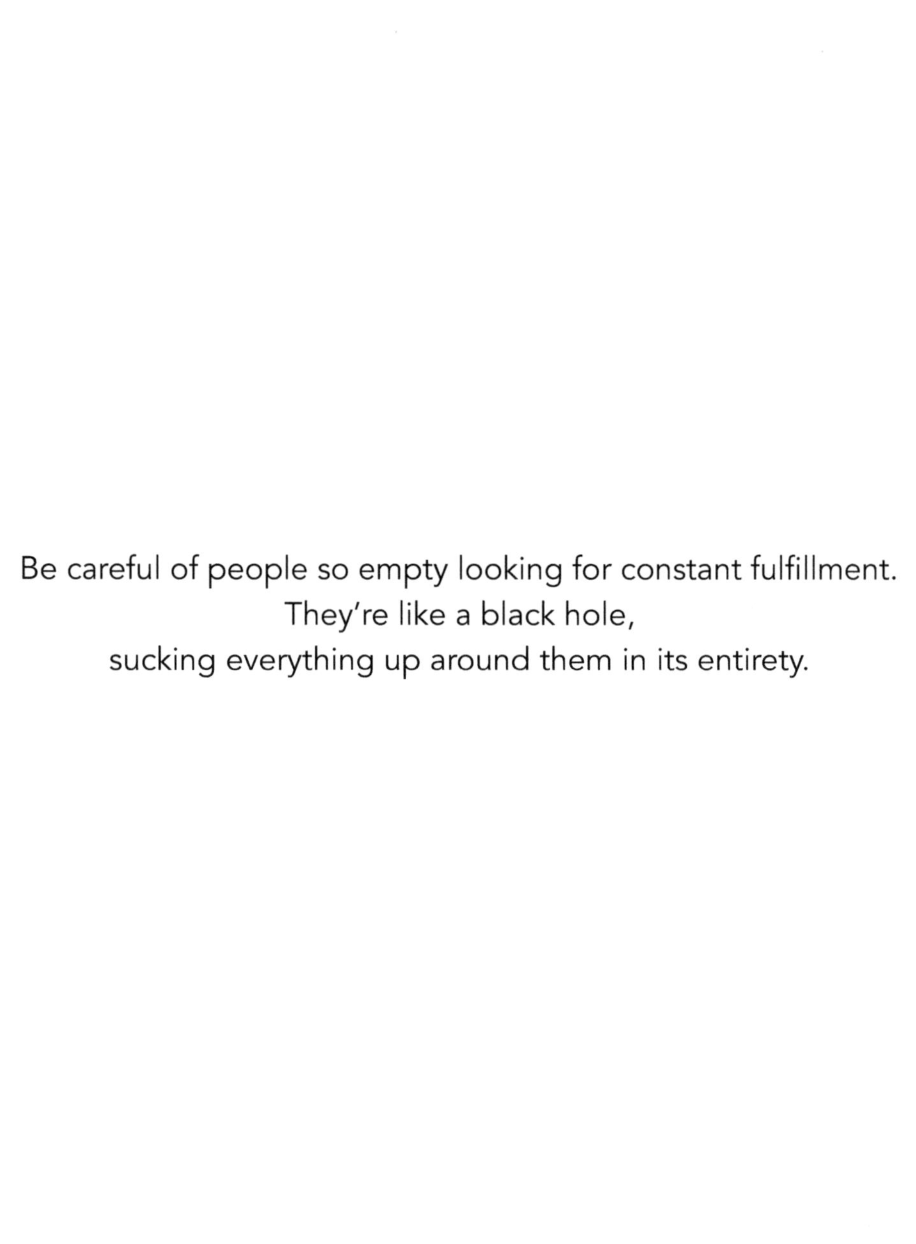

Be careful of people so empty looking for constant fulfillment.
They're like a black hole,
sucking everything up around them in its entirety.

Even if you look in the most innocent places
you can find negative things...not because it's there,
but because you created it.

The number of your age
doesn't give you a free pass to wisdom.
I've seen deep insight from a 5 year old
and have heard shameful ignorance from a 70 year old.

Senses are our book of life on a dusty shelf;

the glimpse of a person,
reminiscent of someone you loved dearly;

driving in the night air
while scents from your memory sweep into the car;

a song on the radio that transforms time;

a hug from a stranger seems so familiar...

These moments keep us close to who we are,
even when our mind fails us.

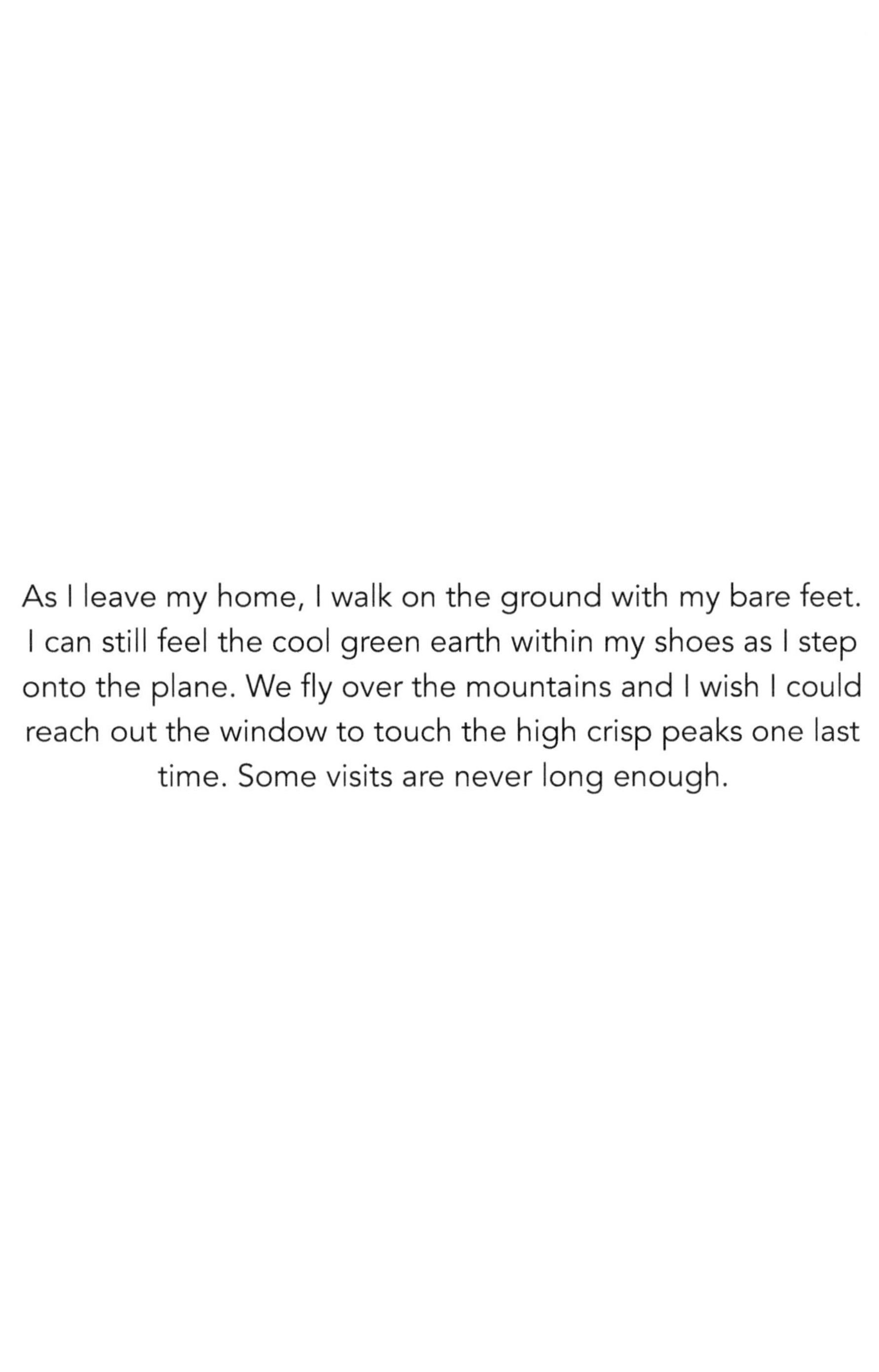

As I leave my home, I walk on the ground with my bare feet. I can still feel the cool green earth within my shoes as I step onto the plane. We fly over the mountains and I wish I could reach out the window to touch the high crisp peaks one last time. Some visits are never long enough.

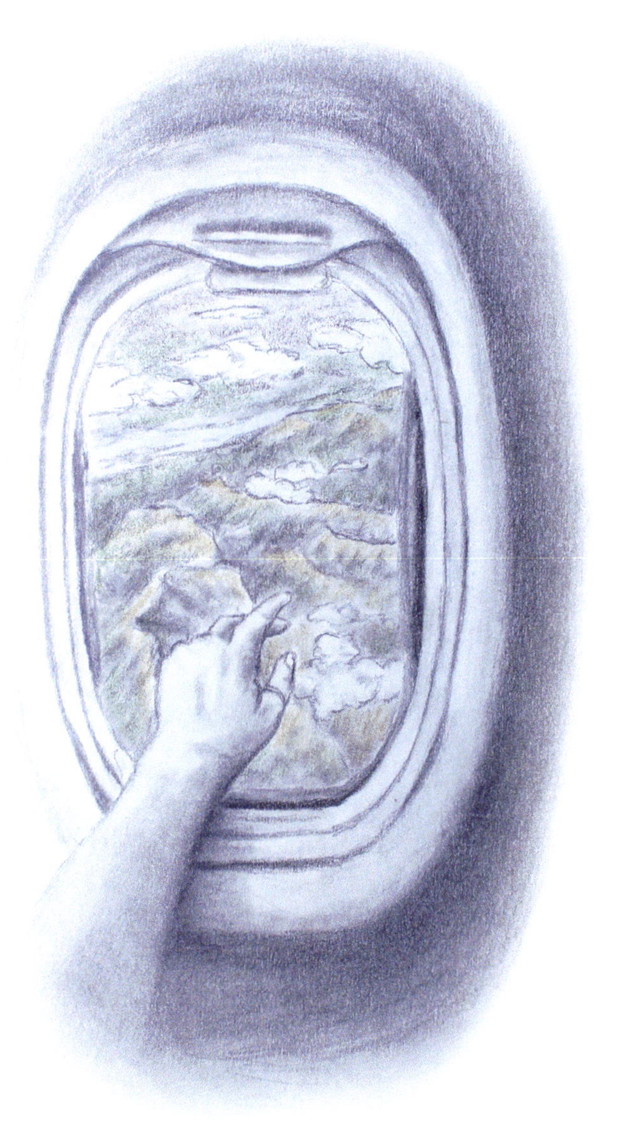

Don't get offended if someone with pure intentions
doesn't talk within your definitions.
Bring it back to simple;
have understanding, embody respect,
and all the rest will be covered.

It is horrible to feel so loved by someone,
to seem completely safe in your love,
only to find out they have hidden thoughts,
that tarnish your truth,
metaphorically ripping the magic rug
from beneath your feet,
leaving you to fall back down to Earth.

An artist's mind is full of complex scattered thoughts,
yet their art can portray a single idea in a profound way.
I guess you could say it's how they organize the chaos.

A lover is someone who loves everything
or wants to love everything,
even the things that scare them.

Too much pride and not enough skill,
laced with judgment and lacking will.

Jealousy is basically negatively charged admiration.

Pain and suffering are the imminent outcomes of unsustainable ways, but there are also unintended consequences that shed truth, a lighted way to empower change before total destruction.

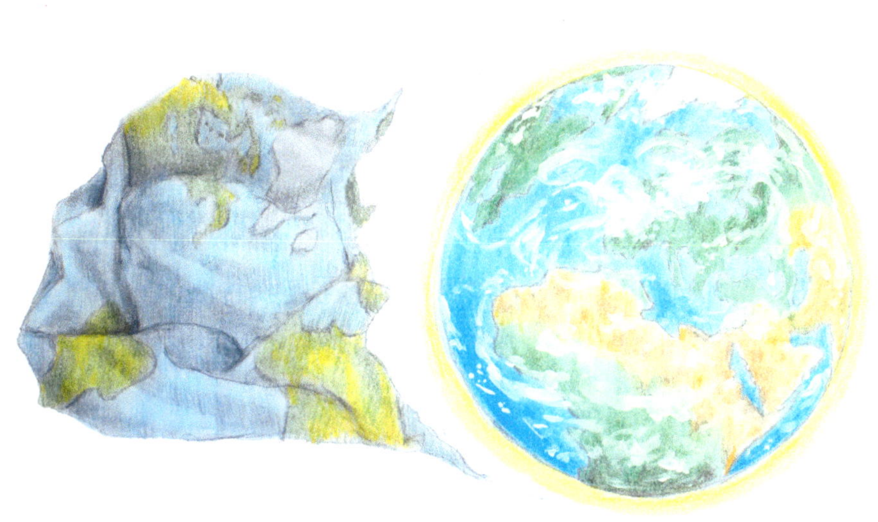

Sky High

Standing high in the sky,
the sweet fresh air
breathing through my hair.
Valleys carved into the earth,
no one knows its worth.
Beauty unclaimed
untamed...
A place of no walls,
only valleys of trickling waterfalls.
Sun pours through the peaks
brightening all it seeks.
Worries melted away,
a place for the soul to stay.

Let's start living amongst many trees
instead of the few living among us.

Live well below your means
and your possessions will never own you.

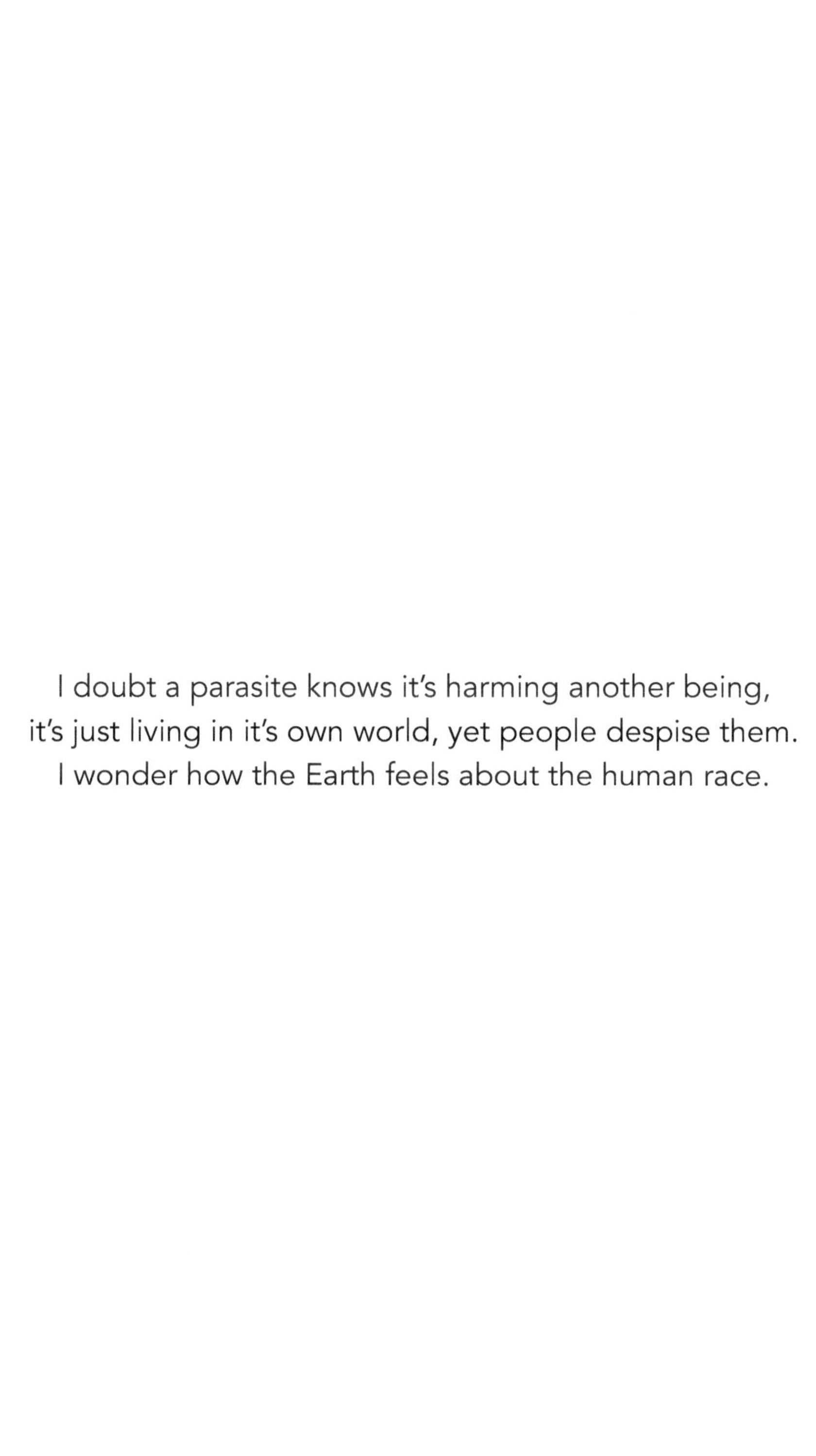

I doubt a parasite knows it's harming another being,
it's just living in it's own world, yet people despise them.
I wonder how the Earth feels about the human race.

They say you make yourself whole,
that you make your own happiness.
But when you live in deterioration and trauma,
you can give too much away;
trying to heal your environment,
leaving no room to manifest
happiness within yourself.

I used to be able to find you, under the addiction,
but that's before you let it steal your sight of me.

Time is relative.
I believe that the life of a butterfly is just as long to them as our life is to us. Though maybe ours is shorter with the pace we live. If we all learned to live as simply as a butterfly, allowing life to morph us into more beautiful things as we grow, we'd know how to use our wings more graciously, being able to glide with time instead of going against it.

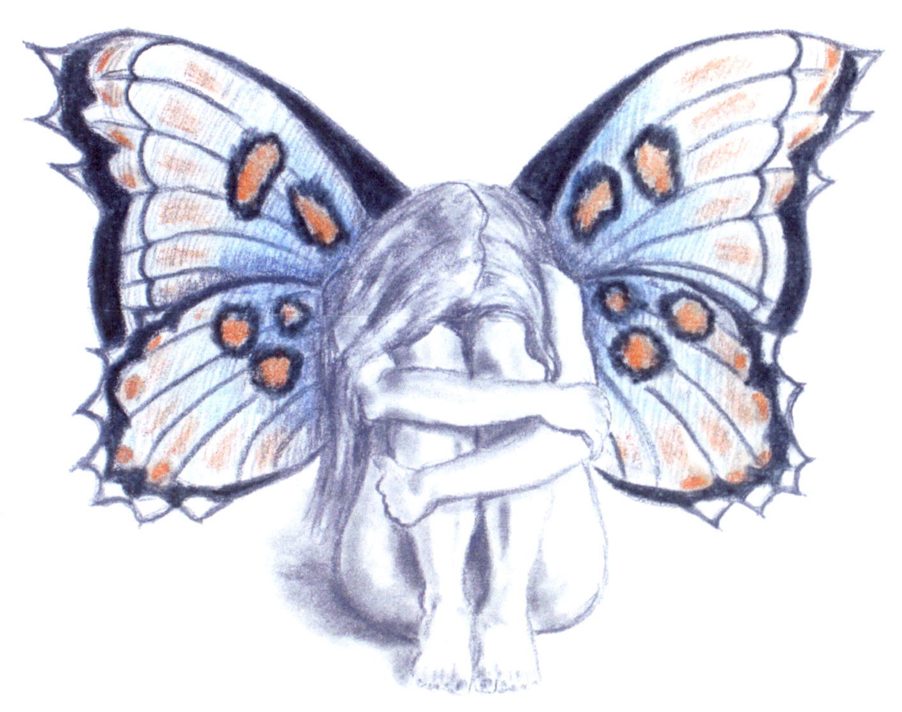

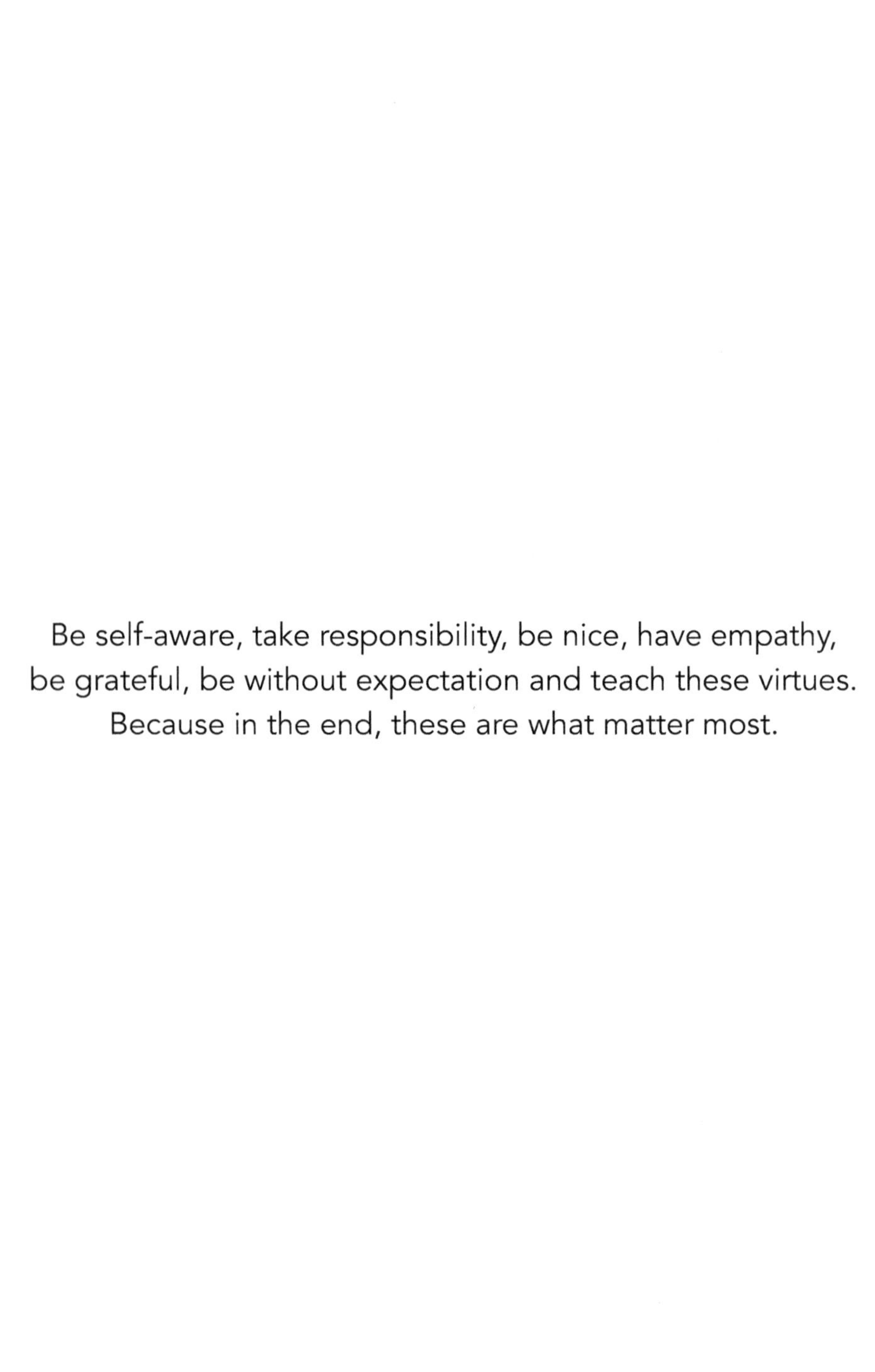

Be self-aware, take responsibility, be nice, have empathy,
be grateful, be without expectation and teach these virtues.
Because in the end, these are what matter most.

www.ingramcontent.com/pod-product-compliance
Lightning Source LLC
LaVergne TN
LVHW052307100826
845147LV00006B/696